PISCATAQUA POEMS 2

A Second Seacoast Anthology

Enjoy!
C.S. Eagu

Piscataqua Poems 2: A Second Seacoast Anthology
Copyright 2023 by RiverRun Bookstore

Edited by Mary Anker, Erine Leigh, and Courtney Marshall

Published by RiverRun Bookstore
32 Daniel St.
Portsmouth, NH   03801

Two dollars from the sale of each book will be donated to support the Portsmouth Poet Laureate Program. www.pplp.org

For more information go to www.piscataquapress.com or email info@riverrunbookstore.com

ISBN: 978-1-958669-16-7

www.riverrunbookstore.com
www.piscataquapress.com

PISCATAQUA POEMS 2

A Second Seacoast Anthology

Introduction

About a decade ago, we here at RiverRun began publishing books. Once we held that amazing, Promethean power in our little hands, we decided it would be great fun to put together *Piscataqua Poems,* a collection of local poets celebrating all the things we love about the Seacoast.

Well, it was fun, but it was also so much work that I didn't think about doing it again for about a decade. In fact, probably would not have done it again if it weren't for the drive and dedication of Mary Anker. If you know her, then you know what I mean.

The editors (Mary Anker, Erine Leigh, and Courtney Marshall), combed through every submission for this new anthology, and narrowed it down to the 100 plus poems you now hold in your hand. From these chosen poems, they then awarded one gold prize, one silver prize, and three bronze prizes. It's fascinating to find in just the decade between this anthology and the last, a greater breadth of diversity and viewpoint in our fair city.

It pleases me no end that the poem chosen for the gold prize is a poem that captures our current efforts to grapple with the past, written by a man who has been part of the Seacoast poetry scene for decades. I think it hits the nail square on the head.

The prize poems are listed on the following page, and then can be found alphabetically by author within the text.

We hope you enjoy reading Piscataqua Poems 2 as much as we enjoyed putting it together.

~Tom Holbrook, RiverRun Bookstore

Prize Poems

Gold:

John Perrault, *African Burying Ground*

Silver:

Kathy Solomon, *Wentworth Acres Diptych*

Bronze:

Kay Morgan, *On the Site Walk: Church Hill Forest*

John Perrault, *Ceres Street*

Lisa Wagner, *Stuck in PNSY Traffic*

Contents

Rick Agran

Three Scenes by the River

Morning, Ceres Street:

To smooth a small scar on her left cheek
gloss her auburn hair
lubricate the ragged purr of her cat
a cod yields his liver

Noon, The Puddledock:

Silvering the dark surface
and disappearing, animal or sparkle?
in the old wharf's slat light
flashes of fingerlings

Night, Memorial Bridge facing SE:

Salt-scarred dory cleaves
in half on the inbound tide
late summer bluefish moon on the river
liquid stars waver under her
hair untucked from behind her ear
swims in eddy of her face
tickles her nose and eyelid
her back to the fish-licked breeze

Boat Out into the Sky

When she kisses me goodnight
I push my boat out into the sky of her wonder.
Inbound tide and warm foamy waves, me
boat, row and bob with waves' cadence.

The bell at the harbor's mouth
tolling toward me across a mile of dark water,
as I row a white streak in the sea
a path unrolls from where we've been...

And is smudged back black with the sea's palm.
We inscribe the surface, unmake a shadow
and always going, are never gone...
Under the late summer bluefish moon on the river

liquid stars blink and waver.
I wrap my toes around the boat's smooth ribs and row.

Hand-in-Hand in the Goose-Graced Dusk

Pumpkin in the Isinglass River bobs like a buoy for a lost boat
Clear glass ring of ice around its middle, like a ring for a wobbling planet

Wisps of wood smoke float by the new-risen moon, blue sparkle of frost
Bare shagbark hickories, golden birches sway & creak, sip at the river

Four Canada geese, cold-chased, form a restless honking chorus at winter's
sharpening edge, southbound silhouettes above white pines, maybe the
    last ones...

& maybe not... a last frantic straggling goose, a moon-thrown shadow
across my sweety's broad smile, for an instant her eye sparkles, darkens
then glistens

Her favorite moment of not knowing: will this be autumn's last lost goose?

Tony Alex

River Town

The bridge goes up,
Then soon comes down.
Such is the way
Of a quaint river town.

Ships wait offshore
Then follow the tide,
Straight up the river
Tugs at their side.

They float past the bridge
As we patiently wait,
Our lives put on hold,
And we all contemplate.

The gate inches up
And we all make our way
Over the bridge to
Proceed with the day.

The old shipyard teems
With our sons and our daughters.
Hundreds of years
Making holes in the water.

Fishing boats battle
The turbulent tide
As we live and dream
By the riverside.

Ships heading out
Pass colonial forts,
Chugging away
To their far away ports.

At night she reflects
A soft shimmering glow,
As the pull of the moon
Dictates her strong flow.

Near the banks of the river
Where the old graveyards lie,
Are forgotten poor souls
That returned to the sky.

Eloquent prose carved in
Moss-covered stone,
In hope that a lost love
Will find their way home.

The sun slowly sets
As we know that it must,
Soon will be our time
To turn back to dust.

The bridge still goes up
And finds its way down.
This was my life
In a quaint river town.

Elizabeth Antalek

Memorial Bridge

The bridge was gone, but our steps remained—
they hung in the air past the midnight chill that
lit our breath on our last walk across—past dawn
and your departure, the weathered boards torn out,
railings where gulls perched, red lights alerting boats...

Lingering long past the girders come down, the whole
iconic form—and the diverted traffic of the following months,
January to June, July, no sign of you. Silence itself dismantled,
from faith to hope to nothing at all—still, if I tried, I could see
the faintest scintillation, there, of impossibly fine-spun gold,
thread from the fabric of an unraveled dream...

Meanwhile, the work went on. At first offsite, then later, here—
the day-in, day-out dedication, brave ones who climbed the heights
to realize it piece by piece—the new bridge taking shape, the lift-span
floated in. Our steps suspended till, above the treacherous current,
there was again a walkway, where we might rejoin ourselves.

Barbara Bald

Walking with Gulls

White-splotched boardwalks stretch before me
as I scramble over granite rock toward my island room.
Herring and Black-backed gulls share my path,
at times, block my progress.
In summer sunlight we stop, stand eye to eye,
ponder each other.

A mother positions herself between her chicks and me.
Birds, as large as she is, wear mottled coats
of fledgling feathers, squeal for regurgitated meals,
prod her beak—insistent, relentless.
Overhead, perched on roof tops amid island scrub,
sentinel fathers scold, warn, chatter in chorus.

Seeking connection, I speak softly to them,
assure them no harm.
Always I stare, memorize their hue and form—
ivory plumage, plump bodies, yellow beaks
with red food spots, stubby legs and flesh-tan feet.
They waddle before me, beside me—another species,
traveling this planetary road.

We share a mutual look, cautious stance, not sure
what to make of one another.
Like a pup, offering its vulnerable neck to another,
I glance away, avert eyes so as to not threaten,
challenge or intrude upon their day.

Wishing I could decipher their calls,
calm their caution, understand their ways,
I will, upon departure, long for these gulls,
miss their tenuous companionship
like I would my own shadow.

Beyond Listening
Ode to Star Island, New Hampshire

The island calls from ten miles out,
beyond the bridge that allows ships to enter,
beyond the Navy Yard where submarines sleep.

I hear it in the caws of herring gulls drifting
    on warm thermals, arguing about who's the strongest,
        who's the oldest.

Sense it out past the abandoned prison that once housed
    Naval prisoners who broke the rules,
        beyond the lighthouse that guarded Portsmouth Harbor.

Feel it in memories etched in my bones 20, 30 years earlier
    when young feet scrambled over slippery rocks,
        trying hard not to crush periwinkles hidden under seagrass.

I swear I hear its music—jazz quartet playing in the hotel's Pink Parlor,
    wooden rockers creaking on the porch,
        the island's buoy clanging to unexpected swells.

Listening harder, I notice its flags snapping like whips in the wind,
    stones crumbling beneath soles of islanders headed to chapel,
        lanterns, held high, sizzling in wordless procession.

Island roses, wrinkled and thorny, whisper about endings.
    Their orange hips already swollen, already ripe,
        forecast change, sing of seasons passing.

Star Island
Off the coast of New Hampshire

Come with me now to a magical place

where water laps slippery rocks, its spray
tossed like gems in sunlight,
where gulls drift on thermals and caw in delight,

where porch rockers creak in the wind
to staccato rhythms and poetry births itself.

Follow me, like Alice, to a place where cottages
link together along a thin boardwalk, lead

to an artist's barn of cedar shakes and a pond
where sandpipers bob to their own reflections.

Enter this place where an old turnstile leads
through low-hanging shrubbery to gravestones
and granite monuments that share secrets.

You'll hear the wail of a foghorn wending its way
through notes of jazz and music of a six-string quartet,

watch the canvas of moored sailboats flutter
like lacy sheers in an open window,

breathe in a palette of color—goldenrod spikes,
purple aster stars and blousy reds of rosa rugosa,
Its sweetness scenting memory.

Sunsets? Yes, sunsets too hover over open seas,
backlight an old lighthouse with history walking its ramp.

(cont)

Year after year, the island will stitch your life together,
leave memories like a string of beads draped
lightly in your palm.

Here, you'll sense your place in the choir—
You will come back. You will come back,
poised on the tip of your tongue.

Guy Capecelatro III

Breech

My aunt called this morning, my mom's twin.
She had been looking up breech birth
on the internet because I was a breech birth
and my mother said it was traumatic
and vowed never to have more children.
She never did.

When my mom died last year we held
a service and, back at the house afterwards,
my aunt failed to put her cigarette out
and set the house on fire. Her husband
waited until I got home to call and tell me.

The last time I was in my mom's house,
with my mom, I steamed artichokes for us.
When we lived in Northern California we ate
a lot of them. "Ten for a dollar,"
she told me dipping the heart
into the butter.

Gone Wrong

The apples have gone bad. Or they're
soft anyway. My girlfriend wants
to save them to make something.
Maybe a pie. Or a galette.

Actually, most of the food in fridge
seems wrong. The sweet potato home fries
must be a month old at this point. I can't
even remember making them.

Tomorrow I'll put everything in
a green bag and bring it to the dump.
A fresh start. This year, this new year ahead
will be different than the last.

Angels

There are angels,
literal angels,
my mother told me
as I pruned her forsythia.

The yellow flowers had
long since passed.
It was a sprawling mess.

I can sense them
all around us, she said
brushing her long,
gray hair.

Jane Coder

A Dream

Wake up
Everything was a mix-up
The tape is rewound
The girls are getting married
And having babies
And are happy
The stepchildren are warm and kind
And friendly and share their
Good fortune with us.
The friends didn't die,
Move away,
Lose their memories
Their minds,
Their love,
Their personalities.
And the small family is alive
Willing to talk and sit awhile
the brother has no anger, shares
a childhood memory bank.
Favorite stores reopen
Streets grow the old trees back tall and fast
Neighbors we loved return
The bad ones move away
And the stomach feels fine
All real body parts
Original breasts
Teeth, hair
No leaks, no tears and
A secure future.

The Stone

I saw a white stone in the sand
at the end of Exit 6 leading to 108 in Durham
from Route 4 which bisects Great Bay.

A massive oak tree with copper leaves
guards the exit, pointing the way home.
Put on the directional and descend.

Nestled in oak leaves and pine needles -
the stone the size of a chestnut,
in the sand by the side of the road.

One day a great blue heron
flew parallel along the marsh
as I drove west until I reached the sentinel tree.

I wanted to reach out and grab the stone
but impatient drivers behind me, pounding
life's business, waited for me to continue

To move on, to do what was expected.
If on a beach I would have pocketed it
When I saw it, I wanted it.

One day, with no traffic surrounding me,
I opened my door and picked it up
warm and smooth in my hand.

On the Last Day

There were
scented geraniums,
vines on the wallpaper,
frost patterned panes
when I sang early morning lullabies.
Now, in the evening
from the neighbor's window
across the street
on the last day
I can see the dining room behind
double victorian sashes
distorted in the panes
in the twilight.
And the bedroom wall is visible,
wall of blues and pinks
paper called Mountain Meadow
selected twenty years ago
to push the bed against
long nights, bright mornings -
children singing on the footboard.
Later we saw the house clean.
They had stripped
all evidence
of us,
porch torn away,
door moved,
Mountain Meadow wall
gone.
Round details in the woodwork
around doors smashed.

Radiators, friends
who had hissed in the night
like tea kettles,
had been robbed
of their marble tops
that had rippled,
rattled
when eccentric cats
leaped up
to warm themselves
at two AM.

Faculty Neighborhood - Durham New Hampshire

Narrow house,
lonely street,
crows picking on
the yard edge,
woodpeckers
knocking on the trees,
curtains drawn by curled hands,
faces like closed fists
peering through cracks
in the shade.

Narrow house
where silence reigns
inside and out.
Ankle deep oak leaves
whisper.
Twilight fades to black.
under streetlights.
Seasons of walkers,
heads low, carry plastic grocery
bags of supper or dog business
near the university.

Narrow house
where feathers fly
inside and out
like innuendos.
Broken apple tree
of missing limbs,
gnarled body.
Laburnum tree
of the sometimes
yellow flowers sobbing
gold coins over the porch
in cone shaped clusters.

Portsmouth Public Library

Not a Zen garden but
still a place of peaceful meditation,
the library, with its
carpeted paths
to oblivion.
Leave outside
sounds singing
while it soothes and settles
a soul beside the windows at the end
of the quiet side,
a place to retreat.

Inside myself
in the green chair -
Through the long window
I watch steeples
of two churches
in the morning light
while turning inward to find
my way outward.

Outside the building
empty playground toys
cool in October sun.
Childhood memories, ghosts
ride the swings, push a
merry-go-round, sweet as
summer with my
brother on the slide,
by my side.

When it's time to leave.
I walk through the door of the library,
toward the playing fields.

(cont)

on herringbone bricks
past potted chrysanthemums.
Small yellow leaves like laurels
line the walk,
honor the place and
lead me away.

Claire Conway

Caffe Kilim

Sleigh bells herald the entry
Caffeine deprived bourgeois folk.
Evil eyes repel
And Yalcin's thick voice embraces.

From dream into steamy bean,
Cream clouds arouse.
Sugar slides,
Sweet sandy sludge.

Turkish textiles,
Worldly postcards advertise
Exotic outposts exclaiming:
"Wish You Were Here".

They are sent here
To live among the wall art.
Pillow laden benches
Dripping in Anatolian flare.

Confections and edible delights
Accompany hookahs,
Muslim crescent and star
And Christmas lights.

You are very welcome.
Global orchestras throb,
Beckoning you to partake
In the Dancing Goats.

Mouth of the Port

These currents flow swiftly
Through the blood
Of a dozen generations.
A residue of salty fingerprints
Sunburnt on the memory of impulses.
Nerve endings traveling
Like creeks and streams,
Tributaries of knowledge
Of what to do when paddling through.
In a kayak on the Oyster River,
Or canoe on the Swampscott,
Between dams on the Salmon Falls,
Being lazy on the Lamprey.
When to lean into the wind
And the spray while sailing
On the way to Great Bay.
They all bleed into the Piscataqua.
It all feeds the mouth of the port
And nourished by the tides,
Like poets by the sight of the moon.
The pull to touch our waters
Is ancient and deep.
Whether our forefathers
Laid their bothers
On these rocky shores
Or worried over their oars in strange seas.
We all can connect and navigate
When we collect our thoughts,
Direct our boats through the coasts
And out of the nautical fog of time.
Find their reflections in our own
When peering over the edge.
Reaching out and touching the surface.

The Piscataqua Loves You, Prescott Park

You can catch first light with a camera lens
On the roses glistening dew.
In morning's stillness you can cleanse
The things troubling you.

Hugged by both a river and trees
The fountain and the boy
And salt of the ocean cool breeze,
Nature's simple joy.

Further strolling paths of brick
Stage in the center field
Then blooming trees and vegetation thick
Hides sights to be revealed.

Three quiet water features framed
By lusty beds of flowers
And for Josie Prescott named
Where thoughts get lost for hours.

Past the home of the Player's Ring
Fields of verdant green
Lead to gardens like a painting
A gift that should be seen.

Cross the road to the burial ground
Or the island of four trees
But always circle back around
Past the hiding fairies.

Checkerboards on benches of stone
Past the southern pier
You'll find the whale all alone
And the view of the bridge is clear.

The Piscataqua loves you, Prescott Park.

Oriada Dajko

Matryoshka

In your world, inside your country,
in your town, inside your house,
in your family...
... strangers came around.
Even inside you...
Language was never found.

Holley Daschbach

The Beautiful Doors

> *Today I have grown taller from walking with the trees.*
> —Karle Wilson Baker

Every time I step through the beautiful doors of the woods, gifts are laid at my feet.

The pileated the joy of the pileated.

First the sharoosh of the wings in the underbrush as I startle the bird from its business, about my own business. It circles away and then back, finds the limbless pole already riven and battered with holes and grooves, begins its work.

Thinking today, about the frog, the snake the gifts the woods offers every time. Sometimes large, flashy gifts like the pileated, sometimes gifts so small I almost miss them like the frog whose body is no bigger than the top of my pinky. Yet there, so alive in his leaf pattern skin. Taking the risk to make it across the wide trail, banking on grace to keep him whole, and well. Safe from large things coming down at the wrong moment upon his small lovely self.

The canopy holds its secrets far above and I am in frequent danger of tripping - my eyes so often pulled up to leaves and branches. So many greens, a blessing on my head as I pass beneath. And you may think it great ego for me to say that— a blessing on my head, but it is not. For the tree people are my people and I am also theirs. Our dearest needs and wishes, the same, a wide sky, clean water and a beloved place to root.

And so I will open again and again, at the wide or narrow margins of the days, the beautiful doors of the woods, to see what shimmers and trembles inside. The cry of the pileated, the sigh of the pine boughs, the quiet crowd of mushrooms, and I will know once again that this too is home.

Oaklands Town Forest

> *Going to the woods is going home.*
>
> —John Muir

It is five o'clock,
not nearly dusk,
and the dog and I
are in the Oaklands Town Forest.

The choice to take the dog
changes the walk,
I know, but I bring her
just the same,
her joy as important now
as mine.

There will be no birds
to spot on tree limbs between
the shimmering greens of July
if she is with me.

Our pace is slow,
but not just because
she is nine and I,
so many years more than that.
We are slow because
we must examine everything
with great care
she with her nose,
I with my eyes.
Of the two of us I know
her equipment is superior.

The tree roots crowd
and cross each other over the winding trail
they are like long toes or fingers.
And I wonder if there is a way
to trace them, this root to this tree.

So many mushrooms
red, gray, white,
and I wish, not for the first time,
to be a person
who knows about mushrooms,
or at least a person willing to eat
the edible ones.

My eye is caught
by color
bright red, a patch of raspberry canes,
and we stop.

The dog leans in,
uses the velvet glove
of her mouth to pick
only the ripe ones.
Some I point out to her
others she finds
with her fine nose
and nuzzles them free.

Not for the first time,
I wonder
if she is the only dog
who picks her own berries.

(cont)

Surely this is great egotism on my part.
There are, after all, dogs who find truffles
box turtles, corpses, all manner of things.
Mine finds berries.

Together we find this late July afternoon
waiting for us
just as it is, not nearly dusk
in the Oaklands Town Forest.

"Oaklands Town Forest" was published
previously in *The LitFUUSE*, a literary
journal associated with The First
Unitarian Society of Exeter.

The Woods Are My Other Church

The woods are my other church. I say this in awareness of the grammatical glitch of the plural woods and singular church. And yet repeat, the woods are my other church. There are no pews, no candles. Music, yes, but mostly internal. The deceptive silence is its sacrament.

Walk in a sacred manner. See the rocks, boulders on either side of the leaf littered trail. Listen, they have stories to tell, of glaciers advance, retreat. Of ice ages. Of mosses they have loved. And roots that have cleaved them here and here.

The canopy throws sun kaleidoscopes on the ground. Mushrooms here, on the trunks of beech, of maple. On the velvet red innards of decaying trees long down. Dear mushrooms. How they keep it all going.

Go lightly on your way. Listen for woodpeckers as they thrum out love, need, possession on the straight and crooked trunks that tower above you. See the nuthatches, how they thread their way head first down this old white pine and this upstart sapling.

Feel the ferns, their fronds on your wrists. They pulse with life. They remind you with their ancient pedigree, how new you really are on this generous ball spinning through space.

If there is a god, she is a great foolish lover of all these things and many more I have forgotten to name here. Sit with your back against a tree. Choose a red oak, choose a hemlock. It hardly matters. You are here among giants. It is time to pray.

Donna Desilets

Whaleback Lighthouse

I think of you as mine,
And like most who love deeply,
Who long to show their devotion,
My photos are rife with images of you.

You are a picture of constancy,
Unyielding to fickle change.
Made stronger through your years,
You are able to withstand any storm.

Your light is both a warning
And a beckoning forth:
Stay away lest you be sunk
But marvel safely at my allure.

Birds of the sea call you home,
Waves caress your rocky shore,
Vessels navigate by your beams,
And the sun rises upon your shoulders.

I think of you as mine
But I surely know you are not.
A sentinel at the mouth of the Piscataqua,
You belong to all of us.

Julie A. Dickson

Slats

Long bridge over the river
connects memory to my feet
as I travel through time.
I mark each slat of wood
Name them for days I've lived.

Walking across a chasm
full of hope or fear,
bridge stands strong
against sway of struggle.
Even through painful times,
it commemorates these
slats of pain and joy.

One for the birth of a child,
another when I lost my way,
there seem to be just enough slats
to count moments, minutia
that brings me forward
to where I stand today.

Touching Stone

Cold, the granite – hard as ice
but as ice melts upon your touch, this stone does not.
Silent lack of echo – the faceless granite waits,
when hand reaches out to touch, it bites (the cold),
smooth as glass but no reflection emitted;
its inner nature remains a secret.
Rough, a granite textured rock
granular and speckled like a bird's egg.
Unlike fragile eggshell, granite endures
unbroken unless from man,
carefully hewn and shaped or
gouged by persistent water's force.
You stand, touching stone;
I, the rock, stand in time.

Vision of the Past

Wentworth by the Sea Hotel, New Castle Island, NH

Between cobalt bodies of water, singing bridge
hums a bass tune, low tide current, boat hulls bump
against ropes and buoys, masts point skyward toward

a looming structure, rescued from demolition, refaced
from scaffolding staged high above oilcloth tarpaulins,
covering yews and arborvitae; workmen restore façade,

appear as worker-ants, removing rotted timbers, applying
white paint, replacing broken panes of glass.
Decades had passed, decayed hulk on mostly barren hill

above the water, sharp contrast to sun sparkling sea,
sorrowful windows wept like so many fallen tears,
forgotten treasure, memories drifted, wishes not yet brought

to conscious thought - heads no longer turned from vehicles
on the steel deck bridge, causeway to island - no thought
of formal balls, reverberated echoes of long-ago banquets.

Rusted fire escape ladders frozen in time, faded white-washed
clapboards flaked over hilly shoulders and overgrown shrubbery,
vision of the past, collected details to revive the great hotel,

bountiful lifeline of funds, renovations complete, new life
to revere memories. Once again, wrought iron balconies gleam
against fresh paint; windows reflect the dark blue waves.

Singing bridge in harmony with the sea, boats rejoice in unison
dance, a Strauss waltz comes alive in polished ballroom, aromas
mingled with the sound of tinkling glasses, toast to the past.

Benjamin Doyle

The Way to the Sea

Tonight, I head through Rye,
for the beach where we once met.

The drive, I think, will clear my head,
but on the coast, the night is coming.
The orange sky has gone,

and grey is the ocean, grey are the waves that crash
on Jenness sands where you once surfed.

What would I say to you,
were I to see you again?

I know myself, like I know you:
The words would slip back out to sea, rise up
like waves,
explode and disappear
like drumbeats

I start the car again,
the chimneys of the rich houses rising into the ashen dusk,

and trace the curving shoreline with my eyes,
study the lights on the Isles of Shoals
still thinking
I just might find you.

Night falls.

I turn home.

Fall

This is the third time in the last day
that I've sat down to write something
that simply will not come.
I might as well be waking up sick
in the night:
I feel sick.
It's because I drink coffee
all day
every day
so that my mind keeps racing,
so that my body keeps moving,
climbing the endless tower,
running up the endless staircase.
The running makes me sick,
and makes me something else, too:
Makes me think of fall,
the first, hidden, tenuous touch of it
that came to me today with a rushing sound
like the upward thrust of a hundred geese
gathering speed across the cold Piscataqua,
or taking flight over Wagon Hill,
spreading their wings into formations:
the formation of something dark above,
dark
like the autumn evenings in my hometown,
growing colder and dimmer and smaller each day,
so that
I gather myself a little closer
in a wool coat and scarf
and climb the tower
to look out over the treetops,
to see the leaves changing.

(cont)

We've changed,
as all things change,
for better or for worse.
Maybe I feel worse
now that fall is coming
and summer is falling
away,
as it does each year in my hometown.
My hometown
is not the same as your hometown,
but they'll both soon be snowed-in,
and I'll pass over the frigid Piscataqua to see you,
to show you the first, hidden, tenuous touch
of how I'm fated to feel –
Wrap us up in our wool coats and scarves,
to go racing, moving
on ice-skates
at Strawbery Banke,
to see our breath,
to climb the tower, to see the frozen treetops,
to think of summer and her leaves,
to look down at our hometowns,
snowed-in, silent, on winter eves
where I'll wake up in the night,
happy,
where I'll wake up on those crystalline mornings
when we'll drink coffee together
and talk of flowers,
of sunshine,
of spring.

Christina Eagen

Curious Son

Son
curious son
be wary of the knowing ones
who disguise hatred in morality

Remember
you were
baptized under ocean waves
attend church in the forest
and pray at an altar of boulders

Never stop singing
hymns of rhythm and blues
and serving humans
because we're human

Please don't forget
we saw heaven
in the eyes of the owl
the night that Papa
said goodbye

Highland Street Stranger

Lonesome stranger
are you not as worthy
of remembrance
as the salted piles
the steeple's spire
or Prescott's blooms

I looked forward to your footsteps
stumbling along Highland Street
brown-bagged friends in hand
declaring *good morning!* at night

I smiled   often

I wondered
were you once
someone's treasure
stolen by sea
washed up on high swells
shaped by rugged shore
left lonesome
                    passed over
your hues too dull
eclipsed by blues
and greens

It's too late for me now
to pull you from the pebbles
wash you of the sand
shine your dull surface

So may these words be your statue
our proof that you were here
a reminder we've been lonely
your friends mine
once too

Peculiar Pine

Peculiar pine sits sturdy
watching over
the fleeting sumac
and ferns

Once your lack of branches and needles
(But for the small tuft at your top)
reminded me of
blunt bowl cuts
falling hair
like falling cones
snipped by frugal hands
that match my own

Your awkward confidence
insistence to be strange
our shared joke
like a wink
across a crowded room

I've watched people
laugh at your trunk
plan your felled future
charge you a distraction
from more pleasant taste

As if you weren't the one!

Who showed the lost
uprooted and moved
the kicked and the bruised
to stay grounded and firm
hold a death grip on this earth
and declare without words

I am not leaving
I am not leaving

Melissa Rosetti Folini

"Take Only Pictures"

"Take only pictures, leave only footprints"
a sign from the Shoals,
in my youth, left an imprint.

These rivers and oceans and bridges we cross
lead us to places
years ago, may have been lost.

But through care and good stewards with loving conservation
have survived and are waiting
to enchant new generations.

Take only pictures, leave only footprints
so the nature of our youth
can greet our return visits.

Beth Fox

Dear Dad,

While packing to move, next to
the Hermes typewriter you gave me,
I find a box of letters you wrote,
I sit down and read them.

This one, like
the business form I followed in high school,
is neatly typed on onion skin paper--
it reveals the times you lived in:

> PO Box 158
> Vineyard Haven, MA
> January 16, 1968

Penguin Publishing Co.
New York, New York

Dear Sir,

      Enclosed is a check for $5.95 plus $1.20
for postage—a total of $8.15. Please send me a copy
of *Essays and Poems* by Ralph Waldo Emerson.

      I look forward to receiving it.

Sincerely yours,
Robert T. Hyde

No *dot.com,* no Amazon,
no credit card over the phone--
just an envelope and 10-cent stamp,
a purchase frozen in a time,

(cont)

like the memory of you reading
your poems on Star Island.
I wasn't there to celebrate--
was far away from the rocky shore,
swallows swooping everywhere.

I'm realizing the effort it took to
simply purchase a book--

I'll sign off now, wishing I could push
the *Send* button and get a reply.

Your loving daughter

Ode to Spring and Skunk Cabbage

Symplocarpus Foetidus
Great Bog,
Portsmouth, NH

I walk along the trail at the preserve,
near power lines, train tracks.
There you are--
odd, intriguing.
I'm told you have the secret
of reincarnation.

First queen of swamps,
subdued in spotted browns,
you send peat perfume my way.
I become one more insect drawn
to your spongy white blossom,
a medieval club, hidden
in secret alcoves.

Like a warm-blooded animal,
you create heat, melt spring ice,
draw me to your warmth,
your pollen, your hooded flower
that has no petals.

You may be called lowly,
but I know you are not humble.
Driven to be first, you
seduce small life around you,
secure the destiny of flowers,
those miniatures stored
infinitely in your core.

(cont)

With leaves uncurled
your scrolls reveal newness--
followed by green dissolving
into air, water, a mass of roots
receding into the marsh
of all the springs to come.

Mary Spofford French

Portsmouth

... has narrow streets
Pickering Hunking Gardiner
here houses crowd so close even
a stiff breeze can barely squeeze between
where open windows eavesdrop
on neighbors' whisperings
and faces turn to peer in
when passing by

Beach Treasure

I stoop to observe this flat disc as it lies
half buried in granite sand on this
somewhat northern Atlantic beach.

Glistening foam hisses

A single sand dollar   life sucked away
by star fish or was it hermit crab
no sign of sea gull attack although

they are among the predators.

The central oris beneath not broken but
here another smaller-still hole near the rim.
These sea-born animals

as most creatures do live together

Now expired alone sun-bleached white ..
not so unlike white linen spread still wet
on grass   to dry and brighten

I pick it up here
        where it dropped
                    from Neptune's pocket.

Alison Harville

Once You've Been in The Ocean
The Ocean Is Always in You

I read once that to escape
a riptide, you let
the water carry you until
it is no longer a fight
then swim at an angle to shore,

but I suspect that's just a rumor
for once surrendered, how
could anyone deny such surety.

On the foamy beach,
wind whipped and sand sunk,
the surf crash call call
calling my name,

I step forward, sink in, cold salt skin,
and feel deep within
the savage pulse
as it tries to pull me farther,
steal me to the horizon,
wash me smooth and
iridescent as a mother's shell.

Even now, months and miles
from when I clung to the sharp edge,
half-submerged in the sea,
the wet drum of my heart shakes
and beats and remembers.

Sea Birds

My skin is my only remaining language,
tender and stretched.

Seeking solitude,
I scale the outcropping of granite
to the island's edge.

I am a speck
on a rock
on an island of rock
in the cold North Atlantic.

The wind blows ferociously.

Gulls pay me no mind,
scratching their beaks like cats.
The gulp of their song is made
beautiful by the accompaniment of waves.

I've brought my darkness here,
that sad old thing.

I open my arms like wings
and let it blow away.

A Survivor Goes on a Whale Watch

The crowded boat surges forward
through the crashing gray.
I'm lulled by the guttural vibrations
of the old engine, of the repeating break of surf.

Dolphins stay near the surface, romp
in the dissipating wake.
The day is colder than forecasted.
I can't be all things to all people.

We've reached the point where land
disappears from the horizon
hastened by clouds and diffused light.
We've reached the point where

every way I turn is a unknown beginning.
I'm surprised by my lack of panic.
The boat slows to a rocking crawl, sways deeply.
What will feed the beasts cycles up.

People break out sandwiches, children dash
from port to starboard and back again.
The stretched sea keeps all its secrets
and a few of mine as well.

Black backs of whales, visible, rolling,
curving in the water. Occasionally a dive
showcases a fanning tale, its distinct markings.
It's been a long time since my scars were visible.

Then a humpback hurls itself out of the water,
breaching the surface, immense.
All that effort for just a second
of freedom from its endless journey

(cont)

or perhaps to rid itself of something.
The boat circles, full of eager watchers.
All North Atlantic humpbacks sing the same song.
Each survivor's song is their own.

Name Five Rivers

1.
The Piscataqua River
divides Maine and New Hampshire,
like the blue estuaries
between what I've lost
and what I've let go.

2.
So many of my dreams
involve water.

The months spent
in swimming lessons
at the school I didn't attend.

The coastal town
where I wandered the streets
of a place so much like home
but not.

The green river,
immense, powerful,
on whose banks
I edged too close
in trembling devastation.

3.
My music box plays
The Blue Danube,
bringing back echoes
of a childhood long lost
until the music runs out
mid-note
in a little death.

(cont)

4.
I travelled down the Vltava River
years back.

In a language not my own,
landmarks were pointed out
(at least I recognized the birthplace
of the poet politician)

and I was poured
tiny cups of strong liquor
till overflowing

I went to the back of the boat
and let the wind diminish me.

5.
Under the midnight blur of street lamps,
I put one foot
in front of another.

This march is supposed
to save me.

My pocket is full of stones.
I drop one
by the side of the road
for each mile that goes by

so that finally empty
I will not sink
when I get to that river
beyond the shuddering trees.

Title taken from Franz Wright's poem *Intake Interview*

Curtis Hines

Forest Bathing

If I let it take me
        the wind   the marsh   my little craft
against the reeds,
if I am moved and do nothing,
        slowly
            I'm looking in a new direction.

Wasn't sure
        who made the paths?
Then I saw   but the Heron
        sees me first, always
            on the next bend in flight.

Not God's plan but the Beaver's.
        I have sinned   meddled with
            creation   attacking dams that flood
            abandoned roads   my trails.
Pulling at the sticks and muck
        and not make any difference.

Now I let my feet get wet.

Force of nature
        spins the prow, sends me
            back the way I came   tangled mass
Now I let it take me.

Daytrip

You can come backwards down the mountain
        where there is no trail, where brush
        scratches and sends you in circles.

You can touch
        the tree no one has touched.
            You can be alone in discovery –

Until you find the cellar hole,
        where ground was shoveled deep.
        Walls of stone stacked on stone remain.

Backwards again
        the house rebuilds itself –
        trees sink to soil –
        farmer plows by ox and hauls the rocks to walls.
        Three sisters preserved, placed below with
        salted meats, by children
        who will not live to Spring,
           and are buried here
                under us now.

Amy Howard

The 1700s Ferryman

Cold wind slaps the face, river racing by.
Hold on to that boat for dear life, you don't want to die.

The tavern is so warm, the light so inviting.
Liquor is a flowing, the wind no longer biting.

The hours soon pass by, full of talk, smoke and drink.
It's time to journey back, the boys start to think.

"Ferryman!" they slur, "Where's the bloody boat?"
The man looks crueler now, hunkered in his coat.

"It's triple the price to return." he says with a grin.
"Either pay up now, or feel free to swim."

Panic settles in, pockets are bare.
The brain is a fog, what do I dare?

The river is a torrent, rushing by my feet,
Waiting for a victim, to drag them down deep.

The other shore is so close, I can see it on the ridge.
"Damn you, Ferryman!" What we need is a bridge.

Suzanne Laurent

Slack Tide

Thoughts find a calm peace
in the slack tide of my mind.
Water unstressed,
nothing moves,
no ebbing or flowing,
    a break in the rhythm of life.

The powerful Piscataqua,
usually so busy,
violently pounding its waters
under the city's bridges,
pauses, before turning direction,
its murky gray currents
         are visibly still.

I float in this space
reflecting on choices made,
and plan
how to re-emerge
taking new chances,
going with the changing direction
       of the current.

"The Day the Presses Stopped"

The pink brick building
is in darkness.
A place that used to hum
With words tapped on computers
to get the news of the day out
                into the community.

Community was what it was all about.
National, world news could be found
on TV, the Internet or on an iPhone.

The sign on the locked doors read,
"Working Remotely."
A left-over consequence of Covid.
Editors, reporters, photographers
                all out on their own.

Not too long ago,
it was a beehive of activity,
keys clicking, phones ringing,
the occasional shout out for
advice on a difficult piece of news,
long nights awaiting election results
              and, always, cold pizza.

Now, there are buyouts,
takeovers and
the presses themselves
will soon be quiet.
The papers will be printed out of state,
              working remotely.

Chris Ledoux

Sea Hold on to Me

I am holding on sickly
Losing my grip on reality
Fading reality
Your love has me
Hold on, hold on—to me

Swimming in a rough rogue vertigo sea
Grasping white-knuckled to a lost reality
And I hold on singularly
To my roughly rode reality
I focus on the hazy horizon
Eyeing you avoidantly
But your shimmering shifty somethings sway on
And I hold on to the actuality
I'm flailing horizontally

My love
Hold on, hold on, hold on to me
While I try to bridge the eventuality

The seventh green barrel breaker wave
Rises with rippled tides, and I am brave
But it breaks too hard, your crashing sea
And you're heeling leewardly
Crashing, crashing into me
Your twisty typhoons twirl, toss, and heave me
Hold on, hold on, hold on to me
My love, hold on to me

Beaten breathless, I accept your plea
And I hurl, my love, swooning
Uncontrollably
On you, my love, my vertigo sea
Hold on, hold on, hold on to me
I am lost in you, my dear vertigo sea

Grace Mattern

Mill Sluice Trail

The footpath opens to a wide woods road
where it passes beneath a beaver pond

an old stone dam holding water
head height as I cross the trench left

when the culvert washed out. An owl
tucks against the trunk of a beech tree

watches me step closer and closer.
He lifts long, bronze wings and swoops. I duck

and turn. He settles in a nearby oak so I need
to pass under his perch to get back

to the path. Closer than ever, he swivels
and eyes me as I step out of his territory.

Bob Moore

Patience

The trees stood still. They knew enough to wait.
They knew that every season wasn't great
for blooming, so they slowed down and they dreamed
of what the light would feel like when it streamed
for hours in the warmth of a summer day.
When asked if they felt cold, they wouldn't say.
But given the chance, they wore a coat of snow,
and waited for the length of days to grow.
They watched the squirrels and chipmunks gather meals,
but never spoke a word of how it feels
to while away the time and not complain,
or worry if the forest would sustain
their young, or fret about the need for room.
Instead, they held out for a chance to bloom.

After the Sun Rose

I watch the seabirds fly toward land,
loosely held in their V-form,
sun still rising, trees now free
of leaves along the coastine,

the white birch even whiter
in the sunlight,
strips of bark like half-torn paper
furl and unfurl.

I step over a stone wall,
lichen-rich, over dormant grasses
and fallen leaves, over random branches,
find my way to a cluster of reeds
standing tall above sheets of ice.

My eyes spot another wall of stones,
follow it toward a patchwork of homes
built on higher ground.

Before these homes were here,
the walls stood higher, fields were grown
for salt hay, for livestock, a network of walls
stretched across the county,
across the state, farming for wool,
for their families, unearthing stones,

moving them to define a field,
managing the walls even when the snow fell,
even when the seasons
were colder than they are now.

(cont)

These fields still welcome migrants,
snowy egrets, and snowy owls,
welcome the snow and its melting,

make room for life sustained
by brackish water,

wait for the next sun to rise
and warm those accustomed

to the short days of winter.

Niche

for Charles W. Pratt

Bend your head down toward the ground,
and find a stone they're clinging to.
You might be wondering why they're bound,
or how they keep their imprint small.

And yet, they're older than the trees—
the ones you often wander through.
It could be they're as old as these
old stones that used to be a wall.

They do it slow. They first adhere,
then multiply at maybe one
one thousandth of an inch per year.
(A year perhaps when growth is good.)

They thrive together as a pair.
And though their work is never done,
one hardly knows the other's there,
and neither do the stones or wood.

They've done it over time. It was
an accidental niche they found,
that doesn't change when the climate does,
and left them with this space to grow.

So, if you had the chance to ask
two species how to stick around—
to do what seems a daunting task,
I'll bet they'd say "Just do it slow".

While Walking

Each day there is a quiet elegance
between the leaves and light, an ambiance
that's hard to pinpoint in a moving frame.

It's easier to find it when we go
a speed that most folks designate as slow.
It's always been elusive like its name.

Its radiance can catch our eyes when we,
while walking, turn our heads in time to see
it vibrate in a tree or watch it play

on water flowing near a tree-lined park.
It dances in the light until its dark,
then settles down before the close of day.

And while we sleep, it breathes a silent song
and leaves us dreaming of it all night long.

Restoration

The blue of the water glows like a jewel,
The sun rises, red-amber, sea-goers
gather at the water's edge, cameras
in hand, some bring a chair, a pair
of shades, listen to the rhythms
of the rollers, soak in the light. A gull
flies overhead in search of food.

On the surface, there is this emerald
blue, beneath the surface, a landscape
of boulders, jetties, sand bars –
sunlight streams like a standing
river over the water,
white-gold diamonds on sapphire.

This is the light that speaks
without words, the light found
in all things, in the souls drawn here,
drawn to see something,
a kernel of their nature,
a quality presumed to be missing lately,
a layer to be restored.

Kay Morgan

Walk to Mill Pond
April, Durham, NH

Mud, the slow birth of daffodils,
sap inching toward leafless branches

while missiles blow up a Syrian airfield,
and a friend is dying. I'm tired

of wanting color, of longing to walk
without a jacket. At Mill Pond,

ice remains near last year's cattails
and I see a water-blackened log

rise up, but then, the log shifts,
dips through the ice, comes up again.

Light rain pocks the pond
spatters my glasses

the scene grows fuzzy. Could it
be beaver, muskrat or some mythical

monster in our midst? In vain,
I try to clear my glasses with

damp gloves. I'm cold, think about
a cup of tea, a warm scone, wish

I had my scope, but a boy with red hair
and younger eyes, can see the creature

is a river otter and while we watch,
another surfaces and for a moment,

they cavort, slip, slide and disappear.
Canada geese swim the open water

their black heads and necks bent
as they scavenge the shallows for life.

On The Site Walk: Church Hill Forest
Historic District, Durham, NH, 2021

The forest cools the air around me as I tramp
the boundaries where the proposed parking lot
will go. Ash trees, in peril from the *emerald*
ash borer, now endangered by the developer, dot
the land along with hundred-year-old sugar maples
whose forebears sweetened the colonists' food after
they stole the land from the Abenaki who first
stalked this hillside for fox, deer, and bear.

I love this amphitheater-like hollow,
imagine A Midsummer Night's Dream
enacted here — Puck and fairies leaping among
trees — rough benches for the audience
tucked around the edges and up the slope.
And I am sickened by the vision of the woods,
clear cut, filled with 1100 truckloads of fill,
spread and packed behind a twenty-foot

retaining wall, sixteen-foot-tall lights,
burning through the night, hiding the stars.
Black flies buzz the back of my neck
and I slap a mosquito that lands on my arm.
At the Planning Board Meeting, I will raise
my voice, talk about the loss of this
cooling island, the addition of pollution
to the watershed of the Shankhassic River,
and the stories this land tells, if only we listen.

Della O'Shea

Healing Waters

I walk to the edge
of the field
where the river
meets the sea,
Piscataqua and Atlantic
in this place.

I stand on the rise
of that shore
while the sun
conspires with wind,
to dry tidal tears
from my face.

I listen to the gulls
afloat on high
when like them
my soul is uplifted,
peace and comfort
found with grace.

Jen Ryan Onken

The Plague as Portrait of a Sister
for Nicole Chvatal

You on the telephone—*I'm ready*
to throw myself off a bridge. I'm losing it.
The snowmelt stretches out from gray

to blue. I know this tender bridge with its white
limpets and cement. The way your toes
grip the edge so hard it hurts. The grassy bank

all bare despite the leftover snow. Bald eagles
and their awful noise. What could inoculate
against this? The tidy nest waiting in the eaves,

the vernal pools, the purple tulips swelling
underground. The dog sniffing out the breathing
moles. Sister, shall we sink by land or sea?

Nothing floats. We laugh because all our brothers do
is beat us up at Hearts. They ignore our parents.
They're always fucking around on boats.

Mother's Day

A giant bird I can't recognize just vanished
down river. Too far to say just what it was.
Its white rump steady, flashing; its wings sails
flapping low along the water and into the mess
of trees. Mother's Day. I've crashed
the sushi brunch for birds. I am stuffed
by cards that say, "Mom, nothing's perfect..."

And what perfect mom could push to tears
the frantic boy looking for his shin guards?
He'll need to guard more than his shins: Mommy's
the one cracked egg in the carton. She took out
the trash, ate the gift, drank
two coffees, wiped down the slabs—

This heron earth, white water, spring grass
and all the birds— I gorge on it. Enough
to fly home. By the river a seagull flares its white wings,
grips its mouthful of sagging fish. Other mothers
watch their sons run back and forth. They're
already there. Texting me the score.

Tidepools

In the palm of a mussel, a universe
of chipped stars. The tidepool's

shades a forest floor: orange
mushroom, chartreuse lichen

the pale white of fallen birch—
a liquid world of shell

and stone. My son's pale toes,
loose bangs, that veil of slate

eyes, a small refrain of me.
He says the colors of Maine

are blue and green. Blue like this
gray stone, I say, and he agrees.

And green like a tall pine,
he says. I agree. Our weight stirs

hardened creatures deeper into
their homes. After dark an ocean

comes.

Falling Out

I don't recall last year's fall, the knife—

the yellow foxgloves wait
            like patients underground.
We touch the window-panes for light,

    a little breath. Mussels close their mouths
                on the out tide. Not one ship has fallen in. But cold
        as any dug-up rusty spoon,

            this bay. When will my father die,
                and soon? The earth's great tumbler won't stop.
        Dulled beer bottles. Splintered
                                chin—

Ring Trail

This morning you opened
your wingspan and pulled
me in, out the kitchen
window and into the yard.
I said, "Did we figure out
the rides to baseball practice?"
and you said, "yes." My chin rested
on your shoulder. I looked
at the trees. Then it was over.

I never got to the top,
just made the counter-
clockwise passage around
Mount A's base,
the dog finding all the
maples and boulders and
looping up and down
the trail like a sewing
needle. Even though
we were pretty low
we found the overlook. How strange
the word *overlook*,
which means to miss entirely
to pass without a glance but there
I looked north through trees
towards The Whites, sky
unfolding into the spine
of something great and rimed.

Karen Parr

Currently

If born overlooking once strawberry-laden banks
in the dead-end of New Hampshire winter
just shy of emerging crocus
alongside still ice-encrusted
muddy-bottomed mill pond
stagnant lilac bushes
barren birches
inhaling initial breath
infused with raw salt-saturated chill

it appears inevitable
that forevermore throughout
a run-of-the-mill seacoast lifetime
there will course an incessant
and fathomless fervent current
of connectedness
with this piece
of atlantic tidal treasure trove

the river itself
swift venous reminder of
all that moves continuously deep within
and propels us
outward to the open sea
   and its vast uncertainty
dispersing its confluence of ancestral echoes

those lifetimes that came before
historical tales of yore sent downstream
via brackish contributory fingers
into expansive estuary

(cont)

the run-off from great-great grandfields
pastures and forests of the Squamscott
gathered amid ripening cornfields and sunset-illuminated
salt-marsh meadows

tugging us back toward
safety of familiar harbor
customary ebb and flow
wondering how much might arise
during the next slack tide

either way
the river does not have time
to perseverate
at it eternally maneuvers around treacherous rocky points
willfully gliding over a granite graveyard long submerged
and ingrained in all vessels
it sustains

John Perrault

Crossing the Piscataqua

Let's let the bridge go up,
the weights come down,
the snow blow sideways at the car...
let's watch the windshield fog.

Let's let the fact we're stuck
up here—north bound—
ice breaking round that loaded barge,
those gritty Moran tugs,

sink in—a sudden squall
can swamp a ship.
We're in no rush. Down there's a view
of what's on deck for us:

The slow white drifting haul
To the black tip
of God's country. Just me and you.
Soon as the gate goes up.

First published in *The Lyric*, Winter, 2022

Kaffee Vonsolln

Dead winter, still alive.
What's a still life old guy to do
on a cold day like this?

Park in the lot, walk to town,
grab a table by the window,
see what's going on.

Snug. Warm... Four little feet—
furry red boots, hats—
two hot chocolates.

Four big feet. Cops smiling.
Six coffees to go...
Two teens, one computer.

Couple in the corner,
hot apple strudel—sharing.
Her fork in his mouth.

Emma's got her hands full...
Snow coming down,
cappuccino coming up—

what's to complain?
Still life with coffee, kids, cops—
my cup runneth over.

Emilio's
—Sorry, We're Open!

The young lady is served ribollita
with a fresh chunk of bread and a question:
What is it you prefer about a man—
his propensity to cheat—or to kill?

The young lady is perplexed—first time here—
stares at her soup, steps on her boyfriend's boot,
knocks a can off the counter. *Young lady,*
please don't be upset. We are all friends here.

Whatever you say, please—say it in Greek.
Or Italian. Or even English. Think:
here we are on the brink of disaster
and only you— your answer—can save us.

She thinks. She says, "I don't care for either."
Her boyfriend smiles. She smiles. Emilio
smiles—like Socrates in the Agora:
Ah, good! So then: ta chrimata paidi mou.

First published in
Burningword Literary Journal,
January, 2023

A Little Paris in Portsmouth

For *La Palette*
on the rue de Seine
it's a trip to Paris. Sorry.

Elephantine,
on the other hand,
is in a Portsmouth alley.

Ah*, La Palette*—
croissant, baguette,
and *café* on the terrace...

At *Elephantine*,
the terrace too—
and chairs like they have in Paris.

You can smell the Seine
from *La Palette*,
a five minute walk away.

The Piscataqua
from *Elephantine*
is a hundred yards I'd say.

At *La Palette*
they quote Pleynet—
and Ponge—with their espresso.

I wrote these lines
at *Elephantine*
over Keats and a cappuccino

African Burying Ground

Portsmouth, NH
for Valerie Cunningham

They dig in the dirt
peeling the white skin
of history away—digging deep down
in black earth for remains.

Digging down, feeling
their way for the bones—
for the paved over bones in the black holes—
for Black Souls without names.

Feeling for what lies
underneath what ties
old Portsmouth to the new: Two hundred lives
consciously forgotten.

Salvaging what's left
of the Black cargo
below decks—merchants on mighty waters—
white sails catching the wind.

Ceres Bakery

Back room of the Bakery,
fire in the grate,
late winter light.

Good to have a hearth,
a cup, a small bite,
close out the day.

Dylan drifting in
from the ladies' kitchen:
"Shelter from the Storm."

Come in she said, look—
Laura's latest paintings
lighting up the wall.

Lonely as it gets out there,
lonely in here
feels more like a little hope.

"One of us is lost," Robert said.
What do you say,
now the snow has stopped?

Penny for your thoughts

Jessica Purdy

In March, the River Ice
After Dawn Boyer's Mood Indigo XI

As if by sorcery, an indigo ribbon shocks
the sepulcher of the river's plaster shell
glides into the soft spots, the interstitial space between

cranial bones, soaks the water of intuition,
spirit-water. The babyskull
innocence of flexible sutures and fontanelles.

Just when we thought the ice had knit
together, its crochet weakens.
Warmth finds the stress

cracks and like a craze of slow motion lightning
begins its slow reach towards release.
Spring is waving us in,

to the safety of a shore layered in a glue-like dusk,
affirming it will come again. Have you ever bitten
down expecting shatter, but felt instead

molten ice, the indigo mind of water, batik blue
dyed cloth-wrapped mummies, brains hooked
out in a line of watery yarn?

Have you ever transcended the realm of reasoning
into the sensed, the knowing beyond knowing? Felt
that bony sheet, calcified as teeth, begin to feather

as a swan, dissolve into sheep's wool?
Insight arrives then, once you stop looking for it—
a birth has melted the titanium milk of winter.

March

It's March and the image of the wind
is a man breathing from the sky.

His is a cloud-shaped head. Blue
and black and white fills the outline.

It's March and I'm biding my time.
If the air could just release me. I'm prone

in the bed dreaming of a shirt hanging
on a line. I'm prone to fits of anxiety.

Any boiled water I drink comes bubbling
to the skin-like shame. I'm learning

to throw water on it before it rages.
I was just burning something in the yard

and the whole county caught fire. Mud
seeped in and clogged the pipes.

Nothing works anymore. Machinery
doesn't think. Like me it keeps chugging along.

The sun is leaving striped shadows.
The snow has been dazzling for so long

the landscape is starting to bore me.
I can't fashion a response to this weakness

in my eyes. Can't say I'm not impatient
for the season to hurry up and change.

But I'm putting my hand up telling it stop.
Someone told me they saw the first crocus.

Its purple petals sharp and curved. I heard
people talking about the witch hazel appearing

and there it was. From my kitchen window
I see pussy willows. When I was little I'd stroke

them against my face and wish they'd turn
into brand new kittens that would stay small forever.

There is Nothing Not with Me Anymore

Memory flicks its tail. Disappears behind rocks. Memory has this brown fur.
What was that? Someone asks. The answer is one of three things, though
I'll never be sure which one it is

definitively. At my kitchen window where I've stood every day I see the
pussy willows are beginning to burst open into leaves. As they did last year.
The dusty screen in the window is like

time. This build up of dust makes it hard to see out. What use is all this
time anyway? The seeds sprouted while I wasn't looking. Now it's spent
wondering when to transplant. I'm no gardener

but I can push a seed into dirt. Make it disappear. The seeds were dry,
white, hard. The soil is dark and stinks of the earth's breath. What wonder
appears on the seventh day. Memory

entrusted to time rises, unfurling, pushing its tender arms toward the sun.
Some don't ever come back up, they're like stones thrown deep into a
summer lake. Submerged like this, the

stones become slippery, furred with algae. The water's displacement is
barely discerned, but can be measured over time—retreating marks of
detritus where it once touched the shore.

To My Sky in Winter

You make no apology. Even though I beseech you
to acknowledge what I'm going through. The abuse

of stinging sleet. The lonely way you mock me. And I'm still here
standing under you. Making the choice to stay and walk the river.

Every reflection lords you over me. My stick breaks the ice.
You are the bird's sidewalk. Do you need each other?

Who am I to say we're done? I can't blast off without you.
Without you, neither can I taste the berries of summer.

So you've given me heat, that's our history. You can take it
away too. Prod me awake with your desire. Where I am

on the planet in December is cold. Even gloves take degrees
away from my blood. I'm a radiator against my will.

Your apology always comes too late. I am so wretched
I forgive you your temperament. Turn my face up to your changes.

Though you've buried my heart in drifts of snow,
your hand on my back is warm, meant no harm.

This Feeling in March

Robins clog a thawed patch of scraggly grass. Six rawmeat colored breasts clot inside a circle of snow.

Once small enough for me to hold the whole of them, my children have grown to ever-widening territories. Wolves or lone cats, they spray their scent on the voyage out, then return.

I caught the bleary eye of morning, red and sweet as corn syrup blood.

Her eyes when she's crying ovals of pain.

Worked in woe I have no more tears. Can't conjure them even with magic.

Steeped in patience I've waited out my sentence. This sentence ends but is transfigured the way transitions mark the space between bodies that once touched.

I named them.

She is beautiful goddess. She is pearl. Youthful and downy. Razored sear of lightning.

He is gracious. God is. Smiles easy as a temperate sun.

When the year moves away from the first month, I can feel it stalking me beneath the blinding snow. What I know of it I can count on again.

Slit of menthol green in an otherwise blue sky. February light. A chlorine pool foreseen.

Shadowed, trees cast themselves out as the nets of fishermen. Slide their slow tendrils
over the drifts. I'm upended.

A cat's white belly mirrors the surface of snow. His back gray as today's sky. In the river, the great blue heron's chest feathers dangle like icicles in the moonscape of thawing ice.

I'm going to start painting my children. Their eyes in daydream, hands deep in the cat's fur, or maybe they'll be palm up, bringing me their gifts.

Ode to Summer Street, Exeter, New Hampshire

That paves the way for trucks that speed
and loud engines the foul stench stretching
out behind and the oil that slicks
and the exhaust as gray as the snow in February
and the plows that lower their blade edge
against it sometimes sparking with friction
through the storm at night and at night
when headlights sneak around the edges
of the blinds and eyelids where the turn
at the triangle makes a stomach lean
and the cat lopes across to the neighbor's
with five cars on the postage stamp yard
and the ruts in the grass and the American
flag snagged in the leafless birch and
remember the red tulips that come up
there in spring and oh the street
that was repaved over the replaced pipes
from 1860 and next door the ongoing
construction of a new garage and my street
in spring that feels like a Peter Frampton
song when the sun sets pink and earthworms
unearthed after a rain next day dry up
in hot summer sun and sidewalks and curbs
for the mail carrier and the strollers
and the mothers and fathers and dogs
and kids on their scooters and sometimes
foxes come round and snapping turtles
lose their way from the river looking
for good places to lay eggs and turkey
vultures and military cargo planes
fly over from Pease Airforce Base
or the Amtrak train rattles through
shaking the glasses in the cabinets
past the neighbor's house where the man

with bladder cancer lives and sometimes
you see him with his wife walking ten feet
behind him and the crossing arm goes down
and dings and dings until the train goes past
and the arm goes up again and the affordable
housing flashes red again with ambulance
lights and the first responders have to go in
through a window to reach the woman
who always calls them and the house
where my friend used to live
before she moved away
and before her house had even existed
a silver airstream camper had rotted
and oh if you turn right you can walk
to town by the river and see eagles
and cormorants and herons and if you turn
left you can reach the highway
knowing there's always this homecoming

Every Architecture is a Mirror
After "Before We Came Down from the Trees" by Kate Knox

I am like a milkweed pod in autumn: my silk wings finally escape,
but seeds by the hundreds anchor me. Am I at odds
with myself or are we a team?
I am like a leafless tree whose roots penetrate the winter white sky.
Whose sweet heart are you?
Ink is positive space. A brayer applies the glint of black like salve.
I've cut away the negative with a metal tool.
I am writing a visual. Branches are hair. There is no ground.
I am making sense of my thoughts, their boards were made
into a house I abandoned a long time ago.
Now I've come back to reclaim what's been neglected.
Can I achieve balance? Make a new symmetry?
Impatience is wishing the future would come
like harvest. The past is already a tilled field.
I'm trying to detach with love but bodies keep
pushing up against mine. I can feel their bones' hunger.
I would love to want to be a food source,
but I can only nourish in theory.
A mirror traces the blackest outline of what it loves most.
When the sky is blank I'm floating. Even made of iron and wood.
I've never entered the underworld
but I've always looked over my shoulder from where I came.
One day the lumber of my body loosened
the nails I had hammered in.
My steps, shattered with rot, had been climbed too many times.
Whoever resides in me halved
and halved again. If you fold me fold me
twice so I can see everywhere at once—all my seeds—
where they were snagged, where they were swallowed,
where they took hold.

Winter Solstice at Daybreak

Early to the party she lends me her robes,
her candy and matches,
lights the dome with dyed pastel streaks—
the fluff of watered down blood
and the crunch of an heirloom egg.
Her hair lies strewn across the morning pillow,
wavy with the bent crush of sleep.
If I borrowed her flavors,
the temperature I'd dress myself with would
be sub-zero, even with her friendly smile
that reaches the power lines
crosshatched against her chest.
She's either a captive or fine art.
The eye now opening beyond a dream
turns away from radical beauty
and towards the mundane. No longer
this baby light, a novelty
that brought my face a flush,
she's weaker now a minute's passed.
Her strains of music wanly leak. The song
cannot penetrate all the opening
eyes behind the wheels of cars, garbage cans,
and even toy trucks pushed by tiny imaginations
that salt the earth against the perils of winter.

October's End

Wind's whining. Shadows crawl under the glow of golden-red relief.
Wild turkeys and the color of wet trees.

The sharp staccato of its winnowing through crisp black shade.
Gray wind beats the black width of bald eagle wings.

Tossed like paper airplanes, peripherally, they're brief leaves—
panicked and alone like the last yellow leaf on a branch

that seesaws down in the vortices and eddies, their edge a blade.
Just as I'm starting out I'm landing.

I dart and stick, vibrate and spasm like a struck squirrel.
Staying safe on a branch even as it sways in the storm—

animal or vegetable or human malignancy.
Cold seeps through seams

the absence of any moving phantasm.
When windows in a house are its eyes

they soothe me into complacency.
Glass and panes reflect and reveal

flame and blame the same name. In quatrains the train howls rain.
Oh yes something hunted hangs from my mouth—

smoke, mist, and vapors rise through the circle hang of noose.
Rain fogs my glasses. No one sees me crossing the street

clash, dash, slash. The basement's curtain drain refrain.
Nothing slow enough to trouble.

Pine needles like pick-up sticks. A great blue heron
in the field, looked at twice and not seeing double.

Lips miss the hiss of caress. My hips loose as
hunter's gunfire unseen. The deer launch at dusk.

Something's left a foreleg dangling from a tree. Its hoof
struck dumb and gnawed in the air—a last leap.

April Purinton

On The Rocks

I didn't really like spring
until I was seventeen
and in love

and only then

because we went to the ocean
when it was still too cold

to go to the ocean

and sat on rocks
in winter coats

voluntarily moving away
from the inland
where it was twenty degrees warmer

to sit in the raw salt air
and get licked
by the too cold sea spray

the sharp raw unbound
exhilaration
of possibility in the waves

Forest Spirits

We bought land in the forest
and had ideas
as parents do

of how your days would unfold
amongst birches and pines

I always loved to be a fairy in the woods
pretending to sip from puddles of dew

here is what I have learned from adventuring with children:

it's best not to expect anything
and just be surprised

I've never been able to sell you on dew drops

but only because you are forest wanderers in your own right

trackers of turkeys
climbers of trees
explorers of vernal pools

not a single moment
in the woods with you
has been a wasted moment.

Along the Oyster River

When the snow and ice start
to thaw into rivulets
that rush below the frozen crust
still covering the trails

and it's a sunny day

it doesn't matter
if the wind feels like biting

I know your booted feet
will end up bare
submerged in clear water
against creamy sand

we'll have to drive home
with the heat on in the car
your soft little feet
pink from the cold

the nights still cold enough to wrap ourselves in layers of blankets
but we'll listen in anticipation for peepers

we are of the Northeast
comfortably juxtapositioned
between freezing and too warm

dancing with the weather
and elements
because it is how we best remember
to be alive.

Children in the Backseat

We drive over the Maine bridge
on our way to visit Mimi

on our way to your Aunt and Uncle's farm
on our way to Thanksgiving sometimes
and beach days

I'm a sucker for tradition
and a special occasion

so probably we'll have blankets
and lollipops

little comforts for the ride
as you all hold your breath
and we look out upon Portsmouth below

even into your teens
I still catch you
holding your breath

as we glide over the water.

Tom Richter

Spirit of Duty

They were rowing out to save another Jackie Tarr
Another wave too tall another mile too far
They were rowing out for the soul of community
Surfmen rowing at the keeper's bark
They never will stop until they make their mark
To save the lives of those at the mercy of the sea

Out into the fury the Surfmen row
From the top of the crest to the trough below
Those who have fallen from the waves still haunt the sea
They were guided by the glory, strength and power
Burning like a beacon in the Wood Island tower
Enough to set the hearts and souls of the Surfmen free

In the spirit of duty Surfmen will row
As they row and will always continue to row
In the heart of the harbor all we can do
Is to bring you home

Out into the fury the lifeboat man
Rows his heavy surfboat just as hard as he can
Rows through the dark saving one life at a time
For each soul thrown in the bottom of the boat
The spirit of duty is learned by rote
As each Surfman puts his one life on the line

Joshua James and his brothers of lore
All heeded the cry of "Ship Ashore!"
When the volunteers had nothing left to give
Now women and men on the deck stand tall
As the Coast Guard rows to the mayday call
In the midnight gale so that other souls might live

In the spirit of duty Surfmen will row
As they row and will always continue to row
In the heart of the harbor all we can do
Is to bring you home

Janet Saurman

Cannon Balls

Breathing in summer and sunshine,
the children of Park Street,
barefoot, dressed in colorful swimsuits
with towels draped over our shoulders,
head down the big hill
for a long afternoon of play on the river.

Once on the shore
we climb big rocks warmed by the sun.
We tip-toe across patches of wet seaweed
gently lifting the tangled strands
looking for hiding crabs.
We scan the shoreline for perfect skimming stones
and send them skipping across the water.
We wade out, sinking knee-deep in low-tide mud,
a chorus line, loudly chanting
to passing motor boats,
"Give us some waves!"

Finally the river fully widens,
filling the beach with water where hours before there was none.
We hurry ourselves up from the shore to the steep grassy bank
and begin our orderly, much practiced line-up:
single file, evenly spaced, oldest to youngest.
We eye the two-foot wide plank
connecting land to the weathered pier
surrounded now by the river's great gift: deep-enough water.

Dares, double-dares, pep talks and promises
fly up and down the line.
We balance our bodies and tighten our muscles,
arms, legs, and feet positioned to run.
"Get ready. Get set. Go!"
With dead-ahead aim, we race one after another

straight to the end of the pier,
and for one exhilarating moment
each takes flight
before landing with perfect form
deep in the middle of the Piscataqua River.

Low Tide in Summer

After hours under the river,
with drifting shadows above
the only suggestion of light,
the mudflats are fully exposed.
The water has moved out and away.
The flats are breathing again -
air, sun, sky.

Green, soft-shelled baby crabs
scurry sideways across the warming mud.
Snails, nearly weightless now,
slide from one spot to another, trails crisscrossing,
to some distant destination from no discernible starting point.
Seagulls fly low over rich glistening mud
full of offerings and soft landings, a welcome change from
rugged rocks, ragged cliffs, and endless dark-water searching.
A great blue heron, still and observant,
stands at the ever-changing edge of water and land.

And under this warm summer sun,
a little girl kneels in the soft mess of mud
to dig deep, her fingers squeezing
the soothing, oozing salty mix
of good wet earth.
Then, one handful at a time,
she lifts the river bottom
from darkness into sunlight.

Brian Serven

Haunting the Streets

As the sun sets beyond the North Church steeple,
An old Mariner watches, weak and feeble.
He leans against a wharf post weary,
And observes an evening act most dreary.

It just might be his slipping mind,
Seers, soothsayers, even oracles may find,
That the tales and lore he read in youth,
Might just be the unseen truth.

For high above the town square, he sees,
Nyx soaring toward west from east,
draping the heavens with her dark veil,
leaving twinkling stars along her trail.

Facing now Piscataqua river,
The rotting wharf posts shift and quiver.
Treacherous currents run fast and deep,
And whatever falls in, the darkness keeps.

A fisherman's boat comes to dock,
Bound to rusty cleat with knot.
The vessel has seen better times,
Now covered with barnacles and unsightly grime.

Since deemed unfit to sail and left ashore,
No one notices the Mariner no more.
The anxious sailors disembark and bellow,
Rushing to portside bars and bordellos.

It's not until a frantic lamplighter appears,
Lighting gas lanterns along the piers,
That the old Mariner decides to leave,
Granting himself emotional reprieve.

It's only when walking the alleys and streets,
that the old Mariner finds needed relief.
With his life and purpose now asunder,
Wandering fills his heart with wonder.

Coming now to Water Street,
Where seedy taverns and homesteads meet,
Ragtime songs ring from open doors,
Echoing through town and to the moors.

Turning thus unto the south,
Where still stands his ancestor's house,
Tucked behind a knotty tree,
As if lost to antiquity.

Hardly more than sixteen feet wide,
And leaning slightly to the side,
The house stands with windows smashed,
Covered in cobwebs, dust, and ash.

All his family have since passed on,
He the last surviving son.
And when he dies his bloodline ends,
Just as the seer did once portend.

Further along down Water Street,
Just beneath the Mariner's feet,
Years ago, water rushed beneath,
A bridge now gone named Liberty.

Facing inland the Mariner remembers,
Like a flaming fire now left as embers,
How the old Creek used to look,
Before it was filled with gravel and soot.

Before the inlet was lined with rock,
this lowland here was Puddle Dock.
Oh, how badly he wished he could,
See the neighborhood as it once stood.

And as if the sky were torn in half,
Sheering present from the past,
As disarming as a heart that aches,
The dike below crumbles and breaks.

River waters rush into the basin,
Filling and flooding, continuously raising.
The decrepit houses, look decades younger,
Leaving the Mariner filled with wonder.

It all appears as he recalls,
Tired mothers covered in shoulder shawls.
Children run amok as if they're feral,
Men watch vigilant for impending peril.

And as suddenly as the bygone scene appeared,
The pond, houses, and specters disappear.
The Mariner stands a moment at ease,
Before inescapable impermanence weakens his knees.

His heart aches a while as time resumes,
His mind is filled with familiar doom.
To never see what the future holds,
Leaves the Mariner feeling soulless and cold.

With head hung low as emptiness reigns,
He marches onward toward greater pain.
Although pacing the streets often clears his head,
Tonight, he must face long-buried dread.

Following Hancock noticeably craven,
The Mariner reaches a park named Haven.
Set just along Mill Pond, South,
Branching off the rapid river's mouth.

Hardly older than a decennium,
Dirt paths are lined with chrysanthemum,
The land stretches flat toward a peak,
Before sloping down where grass and water meet.

Last he stood here by this tree,
His mouth dried, afraid to speak,
He couldn't tell his beloved how he felt,
He never raised an engagement ring nor knelt.

Back then it seemed like he had more time,
A chance forthcoming for another try.
Departing soon after, for months at sea,
Was their ever after meant to be?

When he returned to port one night,
His dearly beloved was not in sight.
And upon her doorstep he stood with rose,
Greeted only by ominous black crows.

Stricken with grief all these years later,
Awful then, though now much greater.
The Mariner leans against a young oak tree,
Wondering what will become of he.

And as if the sky were torn in half,
Sheering future from the past,
The young oak tree upon which he leans,
Grows wider and taller, nearing 80 feet.

Now the tall trees in Haven Park,
Show weather-worn and aging bark.
The houses on streets Edward and Livermore,
Suddenly now appear inexplicably restored.

The familiar night sky is hard to see,
With electric lights lining Pleasant Street.
The Mariner feels as if unstable time,
Suddenly shifts and again rewinds.

Unsure if time's controlled by will,
If only he could make time stand still.
But as the clock hands spin and stop,
He finds himself standing where he should not.

Near where once stood the statue Porter,
Now lines the street a wooden border.
And three houses tower over land divided.
As the South Pond water surges and rises.

An unseen dog barks at the unknowing trespasser,
The Mariner's heart races harder and faster.
From back doors come owners brandishing broom handles,
While lighting shadows with lanterns and candles.

Darting toward the pond's tall grass,
The Mariner hastily tries to pass,
Out of sight and unheard,
Between the pond and Universalist Church.

Through the alleys under the shadow of trees,
The Mariner reaches the crossing of Warren and Pleasant Streets.
Quickly he rushes to Market Square,
And sees things that shouldn't be there.

Where the National Bank should stand tall,
Is the old wooden Jefferson and City Halls.
The square looks completely foreign now,
The Mariner rubs his neck's nape and wonders how.

A lifetime of wandering this merchant town,
He's wondered of life once governed by crown.
From old houses to brick-and-mortar stores,
And generations surviving wars.

As gray clouds form the air grows colder,
Snowflakes fall as the square turns older.
Horse drawn carriages cross his path,
As distinguished men and women pass.

Although this night feels never ending,
The Mariner feels his heart start mending,
When through the quiet he starts to hear,
Merry carolers strolling ever near.

Holding candles and pausing moments,
Their angelic voices promise blessèd omens.
It's now that the Mariner sees round wreaths,
And quaintly decorated Christmas trees.

Windows aglow from fireplaces,
Rosey cheeks and smiles on faces,
The aroma of fresh baked gingerbread,
Lures sleepy children off to bed.

The lights go out and all goes quiet,
The Mariner stands alone uninvited.
The sky clears and from afar,
He sees the light of long-dead stars.

And as if the sky were torn in half,
Sheering future from the past,
The snow fades revealing streets now paved,
And granite-lined, red brick walkways.

The façade of brick buildings shift and alter,
Wondering if his eyes have begun to falter,
The old Mariner sees now that time is sutured,
Perceiving now the distant future.

And from Old Harbour, up Market Street,
The Mariner hears the tramp of marching feet.
A Parade as he has never seen,
Comes forth alive with fiendish glee.

Spectators line the streets and cheer,
There seems there's nothing here to fear.
The Mariner dodges the dancing undead,
And hordes of marchers who've appeared to have bled.

A ghostly woman with wounded throat,
Mistakes the Mariner's breeches and frockcoat,
As a clever costume and with smiling charm,
She takes the Mariner by the arm.

Through the square and down the block,
He hopes the festivities never stop.
Traversing State Street back to the east,
Suddenly the cheering and laughter cease.

All the ghosts and ghouls freeze in rows,
Standing like silhouettes of tattered scarecrows.
The ghostly woman then releases his arm,
At the ring of a frantic fire alarm.

And as the marchers turn to smoke,
The Mariner hears children cough and choke.
Over by the crossing of Court and Church,
In nearby trees crows swoop and perch.

With fire spreading because of the wind,
Distressed house-dwellers rescue their kin.
Neighbors brave scorching flames and smoke plumes,
To save each other's treasured possessions and heirlooms.

Since a boy, like all children he'd learned,
Of the 1813 fire, where the whole town burned.
It's something he hoped he'd never witness,
Not in his lifetime nor at a distance.

And quickly ever the clock's hands turn,
Until the last structure by the river burns.
From where he stands on Pleasant Street,
The Mariner can see the lights of Kittery.

Walking east amidst the rubble,
Exhausted and grieving townsfolk grumble,
And as sullen man points and decrees,
The Mariner sees, "a forest of naked chimneys."

Heading back to the wharf again,
Where this feverish night began,
The Mariner's spirit has diminished,
But Father Time is not yet finished.

For when the Mariner reaches Piscataqua river,
From deep within his bones he quivers,
The land is no longer lined with docks,
Nor can he see the tidal rocks.

It's dark it's true but what he sees is clear,
An immaculate park has replaced the piers.
He passes granite posts and a fence of iron,
And before him stands a memorial fountain.

Within the glistening fountain water,
Stands a spearfisherman – a river marauder.
Yet it's what's below that causes the Mariner surprise,
A bronze portrait relief with familiar eyes.

Just weeks ago, was when he'd last seen,
Ensign Hovey who'd just transferred to the Asiatic Fleet.
Standing in awe, it would be a lie,
That the Mariner wasn't shocked that the Ensign had died.

Crossing wet grass, through arrays of flowers,
The Mariner raises his collar against misty showers.
Everything and everyone he'd ever known is gone.
Oh, how he wishes for the dawn.

It's not until he crosses Prescott sisters' lower fields,
When just how much has changed is revealed.
Far to his right still standing he sees,
The flagpole named Liberty.

For when he passed by an aeon before,
The Liberty pole stood alongside the shore.
Hundreds of feet of land now stands between,
His beloved river and the old Creek.

And now in the distance the Mariner sees,
The plot of land where his boyhood house used to be.
Nothing stands there no more.
There's nothing left for him along this modern shore.

Reaching the park's edge, he's surprised to see,
It runs right up to Mechanic Street.
And as in his time, across the way,
Lies quietly, the Point of Graves.

No longer are the burial grounds overgrown,
With toppled and forgotten headstones,
All along the stonewall the Mariner surveys,
As through the night breaks the morning's rays.

A great shadow is cast across the lot,
Yet through tree-cover, sunlight illuminates an unmarked plot.
The Mariner climbs over the stonewall and knows,
That this is where his body goes.

And as his essence returns to nothingness,
His tattered soul will writhe in restlessness.
For all the things left unsaid and undone,
Will haunt him until he wakes not by night but by sun.

Katherine Solomon

Wentworth Acres Diptych

1.

My tiny bedroom in the middle
of our four-unit housing block
in Wentworth Acres looked out
over a wild domain, mine
by roaming rights, beyond
a backyard filled with clotheslines,
where clean sheets, towels,
Dad's work clothes, my brothers'
dungarees—we didn't call them
jeans—and dozens of diapers,
flapped in the breeze. Past the laundry,

through a sloping stand of blackberries,
a diagonal dirt path led us
across a feral field where black
and yellow spiders strung
their circular webs from blue corn-
flowers, buttercups, cinquefoil, vetch,
Queen Anne's Lace and blue-eyed grass.

We were half-wild ourselves, children
of the working poor. We wore
hand-me-down dresses and coats,
but we had new shoes two times a year.

Over the hill, on the other side,
beside the school with creaky swings
another field stretched out away
from a shallow stream full of blue flags.

We spent hours there, crabwalking
through nebulas of sweet wild strawberries,

enough to fill our Melmac cereal bowls
three times a week. Sometimes the boys
stole apples from the trees that grew behind
the tidy homes along Woodbury Avenue.

We wandered the woods that bordered
the fields, swung above a shattered granite ledge
on the perilous—forbidden—Tarzan swing.

Deeper in the woods, down narrow paths
through spreading junipers, we searched out
patches of lady's slippers, jack-in-the-pulpits,
and dog-tooth violets. What did we know then
that we only ever picked the yellow ones
with spotted leaves, and left the others
there in the shade in the spongy ground?

The woods opened to a glittering swamp
we skated on in winter, carefully skirting
the cattailed edges until we heard the shrill
of my father's two-fingered whistle at dusk,
whee-oo-wheet, calling us home for supper.

It's all gone now, all buried beneath
four lanes of traffic from downtown
to the malls that stretch over what once
was Frink's farm, Rip's ice cream stand,
a little pond with real live swans. Gone too
the moms in their flowered house dresses,
the dads coming home from the shipyard
with their domed, black lunch boxes
at the end of the day. Gone their troops
of sweaty-headed children, bellies full
of sweet berries, pilfered apples.

2.

Most of my childhood memories
glitter like mica chips in sand.

But more than once I watched
my mother chase two small boys

away from our garbage cans, boys
with lice-shaved heads, clothes

ill-fitting, shoes too-small or too-
big, no socks, brothers, I thought

from way down Rockhill Avenue,
hungry, and foraging for food. *Why*

can't you give them something,
an apple or some bread, I begged.

Because we barely have enough
to feed ourselves, she said. I guess

she never heard how all over
the world poor people who have

the least to spare are the ones most
likely to share what little they have.

Marcella Spruce

Seagulls Have Facial Recognition

The gulls? They own this town.
They know our faces and our secrets:
cross-species small talk is their A game.

They drop a whole crab shell on the bridge just to share.
They swoop in to join our visits at the crowd of names
huddled in etched silence on the brick circle,

the names that wait for us, the ones who come by daily,
bringing the dog to say hello to mother, leaving small stones for the father.
The gulls—such good parents, the scientists say—croak approval.

We are each other, waiting for the ships and following the tides
in search of sustenance, swinging by the bakery in the alley,
stopping at the candy shop, passing by the patio at the bar,

and circling the retrieved granite pilings in ancient ritual
to say "Honor, Protect, Remember"
to the breathless and wingless waiting for us in chiseled brick.

But the gulls—

always wiser than the scientists—

rise upward to curse on our behalf.

Rosemary Marshall Staples

Kumatage

I'll never get over this star I'm
under
on this shoal of land and
sea
Isle of delight, arts and songs
where souls share and spirits meet.
where memories and moments come alive
on these shores of stone and sky
Star Island a gift we wish upon
return again to sing along:
you will, you will come back, you will, you will come back.
Chapel lanterns, and smiles shine bright
Kumatage shimmers its
light.
Dreams linger, each visit's like the first,
a sunrise about to burst.
Star Island is my spirit's home
welcomes you, me and everyone,
inspiration's for anyone
enter Star Island's Spirit's Home
make Star Island your Spirit's Home,
You will, you will come back, you will, you will come back

*Kumatage: A bright appearance in the horizon
under the sun or moon, arising from the reflected
light of those bodies from the small rippling
waves on the surface of the water.

Jeff Stern

Six haiku about an interrupted walk across the Memorial Bridge

The bridge made me stop.
Standing with the others, we
admire our gem-town.

When the bridge goes up,
everything slows down. We bob
in place, like tug boats.

Active and passive,
we stand astride states, abridged.
Maine and New Hampshire.

The Piscataqua:
Deeper than deepest trouble,
fast as childhood.

Massive ship from Spain
unloads Flamenco dancers
and bulls for Portsmouth.

The cold steel descends.
Life resumes. But we carry
the bridge-pause with us.

Nancy Stewart

Salt

Was it first known   as a crusty line   across a brow
left behind   from what was   perspiration
evaporated between crepuscular   beginnings and ends?

All day   hunting and   gathering
two bound   by want   or a practical need
for heat   once the sun went down?
.

Who wouldn't lick sweat   made of salt
off every taut   surface   of skin
then notice   another time   that same line?

Was it first known   as a crusty line   left by an ebbed
tide   along a tan   strand   of fine sand
when such things   remind   us   to find a thread

back   to a taste?   Was it first known   as salt?

Alice Lee Timmins

Puddle Dock Cottages

Airy streetscapes
stretched on canvas,
tilted simplicity,
captured grace.

Shingled cottages
lavender tint,
shortened shadows
implying noon.

Spare palette
Naples Yellow,
one teal line
defining shore.

Pale chimneys,
nowhere particular,
somehow spectacular,
everywhere New England.

~ Inspired by Patrick Healey's
architectural paintings, all spare,
modern version of the historic buildings surrounding
Puddle Dock, now the green commons of "Olde Strawbery Banke."

Breathing Underwater

Out on The Isle of Shoal's windward rocky ledge,
I don't remember crossing here
There may have been a boat.
I float along a sandy trail,
fog polishing the dawn,
Pull and collapse of an old chant:
a bell buoy moaning on a wide wave swell.
Gulls tip and etch the air,
leathery black cormorants dip and disappear
The *sploosh* of an oar
An empty white dory glides in from the mist
I take the risk.

At a beach outcrop between cliffs
my feet cool in a receding wave,
liquid sand rushes beneath my heels,
I'm sliding backward   - somewhere deeper.

I wade out
The chance meeting of an Adonis figure,
An unknown twin? A brother, or a lover,
or both?
We tread calmly
become rose with the sunset,
dip in unison below the surface,
speak secrets breathing underwater.
Coral rays play through him
as he dissolves in the watery indigo,
Memory? Fantasy? – I don't know.
There is a song coming from the dock,
Lucid and back on land
I peer back at the Thomas Laighton tour boat
Loading returning day visitors
I think my way out of my hiking clothes,
dive deep
and grow fins.

Tammi Truax

"Sorry, The Bridge Was Up."

You see the light turn red on approach,
hear the ding-ding of the lowering safety gates
and feel a momentary instinct to rage like the river,
not wanting to be late for something, not wanting
to be made slight by Irving Oil or some such.

You roll your windows down, lean back,
take in the pretty backdrop in every direction,
let the cool cross breezes comfort you, breathe deep
as you watch the tugs demonstrate polite patience,
gracefully, and oh so slowly, showing the visitor out.

You let the cormorants grunt and the gulls screech, waiting
for the final bell, the gates to rise, the light to turn green,
and the lesson to lodge itself in your psyche, again,
as you make your way cross the Piscataqua,
pressing the accelerator ever so gently.

Julie B. Veazey

This Barn

On a chilly October morning up north,
fog settles in the valley behind this 1820 barn.
Built from the dreams and ambition of an early settler,
it once had a hard-earned grace about it,
an ode to the man who needed a barn, farmed
his acres, tended his herd, provided for his family.
Now it decays in solitude, shedding shingles of burnt sienna,
where geometric shafts of light once shone through
chinks in the walls, moved down the bales of hay,
across the stalls and stables, where tittering sparrows flew
through heavy-timbered rafters that rose upward
and bats dipped and whirled in its cathedral.
The barn leans, collapsing on itself. The roof
is crushed from the weight of snow, its cupola teeters,
a forsaken crown. Buckling walls of wide plank boards
bearded with splinters, hand hewn beams,
twisted mortise and tenon, age-rippled timbers,
hundreds of board feet tumbling into a bier of silvered wood.
This barn's time has passed, its essence forever lost to history.
It is survived by a crumbling fieldstone foundation,
stone walls, fields gone to woods, Queen Anne's Lace,
and a deep musty smell of old hay and manure, trodden
to dirt in the barnyard. The silo stands alone.

Odiorne Point

The dirt road is speckled in bronze, trees lay their shadows across my path
and a cool finger slips under my damp shirt. Flower heads shake their
    contents
over me and burrs cling to my clothes. Milkweed pods burst open together;
thousands of small, silent explosions repeat themselves in salvos.
Clouds of silken down drift about like smoke in the crisp, early morning.
Ropy vines of shallow roots, gold-dusted lichen over stone,
spangles of light float graceful as the water rises around a rock.
A small portion of the sky scribes designs of celestial calligraphy.

Deer

Tawny brown hide and outward curving antlers,
a deer stands in the middle of the road, his short tail
flicks from side to side, he's alert but not alarmed.
I slowly bring my car to a halt. He raises his head,
black tipped ears swivel, he turns to regard me
with dark liquid eyes. As I lean from the window,
his muzzle lifts to my scent.
I am mesmerized by his grace and the delicacy
of his legs bathed in golden light and purple shadows.
He takes fright, breaks into sudden long stretching leaps
that defy gravity, that are like water shooting over a falls,
that are like ballet. In one smooth flowing motion,
he disappears into the underbrush, and, in the field beyond,
leaps high above the grass.

Mount Major

At the base of the mountain,
we are drawn into the cool pine woods.
Autumn air fills our lungs;
we climb past weeds and thistles,
rotted rust-brown leaves, red boxberries
and lichen-covered rocks. Exhilarated,
I reach for saplings to pull myself up.
Below, the amber light of October
rests on fields and meadows and ponds.
Mist settles at a mountain stream
where we rest by the winding trail.
I slip my hand into rushing olive-green water,
choosing a satin stone. Chills run up my arm.
Stretching flat on star-tipped moss,
I drink and watch the water carry away images
of slanting sun rays reaching through the naked trees.
Wind whips across the peak as we reach the rocky summit.
Sunlight filters into the valley below,
like summer's last benediction.
A flock of birds flies high above us,
beyond the tallest tree tops.
My spirit soars with them.

Blizzard

From my apartment on the 4th floor,
I watch the snow falling in swaths past the window,
certain and constant, building drifts on the narrow deck.
It drapes over the trees below like wet laundry
drifting through the streetlamp's bell of light.
In the distance, garlands of snow lace the spire of the North Church.
Deepest evening darkness presses against the window,
the crystal blue of air made hard and pure by cold.
In a time warp, it hurls me through a space I do not know
and I shiver from the cold and at the thought of not knowing.

Lisa Wagner

Stuck in PNSY Traffic

Kittery's heart
contracts and releases
according to the hour.

Vehicles
course through
ventricles
and surge through
the aorta.
Colossal trucks,
loud
with throbbing pulse,
intimidate
cars with lone commuters.
Buses
aspire
to lower the pressure,

and yet

Government Street –
blocked.
Whipple and Walker –
hardened arteries.
The venae cavae –
State and Shapleigh –
have acute occlusions.
Even little Love Lane –
connecting capillary –
its valve closed to avoid
a viscous clot.

Years
separate me from the busyness
of the world of work.
Yet here I
idle idly –
immersed, immobile, downbeat –
as the town's lifeblood
strains to flow from
lung to heart to body
and from
body to heart to lung.

Katie Wentworth

The Heron

Black thoughts piling up
I stopped to watch
a long-legged bird
standing stiffly
in the marsh grass.
Eyes striped in black
head pivoting
Sharp beak searching for a morning meal.

Great is true
Heron is right
Blue is ...
Blue is wrong.
This heron is black and white and gray
No blue.
No matter.

She made me smile,
this gentle bird.
We were a natural pair.
I was no longer blue at all,
And she was never there.

Nancy Wheaton

Crossing

In those long gone days of my bridge fear
you took me to see, *just look.*
Talked to me. "See the tunnel? Trains carried supplies
over the river to the shipyard. New York City passengers
in forward cars traveled to the big hotel."

I park across the street. Gaze over,
remember. The university sent you
to Brazil for a water project. You wrote
every day. Until that Saturday. Lutescent,
that metallic sun shining through the hollow shaft.

A lifetime ago, you said: *"just look.* No hurry.
Did you know the water is deepest nearer
the shore? See the eddies forming?" My stomach quivered.
Traffic stopped on the highway, overhead.
Fear, like a sudden rain, dripped down my legs.

One summer evening, full moon radiant above us, I decided.
Whispered, "One more look." We sat in the humming silence.
At 5:00 am we drove over. Got out on the other side. Water
swirling, water welcoming. You drove us back, laughing.
Where are you now? Do you still love me?

Last night I dreamed I glided over river steadiness.
I flew through the passageway. No cars, only the haloed lights
of the other side. A crane leaning over the water's edge, like a sentry.
Nearly a full moon. I crossed over, content.
My spirit, like that tunnel train, soaring through.

On Visiting

You must remember that nothing is as we
see it swirl in our mind – those days
of running to see snow falling out the window,
deer crossing the backyard. Watching shadows
deepen, spread. The delicious quiet.

You did not know their despair; mom cleaning
always cleaning something, dad flipping
through bills. Smoking. They sold their
unmanageable sadness; bought a small two-bedroom
hopeful in a cul-de-sac in Florida.

You travel to the Greenland farm after the blur
of your high school reunion. You tread on
your marble memories. The stars rise
as you walk to the door. The new owners smile.
Invite you inside. They have painted over the smoke odor.

You see their sunny yellow dreams come to life.
You realize that everything matters. Houses
have iterations. Upgrades. You baste stitch memories
together. Leave remembering in the summer moonlight
mom and dad alone in their immaculate anguish.

You stop at the Wallis Sands pullover. The water is gray-green
and calm. You feel full as if you have eaten salmon
prepared over an open grill with dill and truffle butter. Solid,
steady ground awaits as you exit the car. Walk to the edge of the water.
Smell the sea. Glean your miniscule part, know you are attended.

Jack Witthaus

Hampton Falls River Bridge

Hampton Falls River Bridge
The steel of the *Eastern*
Crawls from Seabrook underbrush
Brushed by windswept salt marsh bulrush
To step over Hampton tides

Abutted by granite's eternity
Sturdy against time,
Locomotive's hammer at speed
Portland Express shuddering girders over patient water
7 cars, 14 trucks, 28 axles clattering over rail ends at speed
Airline double track
Trembling promise of forest, river and sea
Shaking gunmetal shards to rest face up in the mud

Staring as the summer trains swell and fade, the freight grows and
    disappears,
Maine famous potatoes, milled goods and manufacturing,
pouring through Portsmouth and away,
Past becomes storied, then sullen
the rails grow quiet

One track remains to bear witness to the the bright future a reactor's waste
    away
Granite sturdy, girders rust red bright and trackless, shedding metal
strength to paint the muddy
marsh floor
witness to the passage of time and innumerable trains no more
Now laid to rest
Spanning Hampton water
Outlasted only by the tides